A MOTHER'S LEGACY

JEANNE HENDRICKS

NAVPRESS
A MINISTRY OF THE NAVIGATORS
P.O. BOX 6000, COLORADO SPRINGS, COLORADO 80934

The Navigators is an international Christian organization. Jesus Christ gave His followers the Great Commission to go and make disciples (Matthew 28:19). The aim of The Navigators is to help fulfill that commission by multiplying laborers for Christ in every nation.

NavPress is the publishing ministry of The Navigators. NavPress publications are tools to help Christians grow. Although publications alone cannot make disciples or change lives, they can help believers learn biblical discipleship, and apply what they learn to their lives and ministries.

Second printing, 1988

Scripture quotations in this publication are from the *Holy Bible: New International Version* (NIV). Copyright © 1973, 1978, 1984, International Bible Society. Used by permission of Zondervan Bible Publishers. Another version used is the *New American Standard Bible* (NASB), © The Lockman Foundation 1960, 1962, 1963, 1968, 1971, 1972, 1973, 1975, 1977.

Printed in the United States of America

FOR A FREE CATALOG OF
NAVPRESS BOOKS & BIBLE STUDIES,
CALL TOLL FREE 800-366-7788 (USA)
or 800-263-2664 (CANADA)

CONTENTS

DEDICATION

Cheerful harbingers of tomorrow are arriving—my grand-children. God gently took the first one just prior to his scheduled arrival. But then He sent Alison, who at age nine embodies everything tomorrow should be—alive, alert, capable, and ardently in love with God and everybody He made. Twins Megan and Lauren make tomorrow believable with their fresh, uninhibited, joyful toddler enthusiasm, along with their cousin Brittany, who is a bright and beautiful splash of springtime. Most recently the animated gusto of little Kristen has caused us to renew our thanksgiving for the lovingkindness of our heavenly Father.

These pages are written for them—and for countless others yet unborn to believing mothers who may be impacted by these words. Hopefully, tomorrow's children will know that thinking Christian women, perched on the rubble of the twentieth century, really cared about them.

AUTHOR

Jeanne Hendricks moved from Philadelphia to Dallas as a bride. She planned to serve the Lord in ministry with her husband, Howard, and to enjoy children as a supplement to her life. Instead, she discovered that motherhood formed a major portion of her real-life education. Four children, four in-law children, and five granddaughters presently make up the teaching staff for her on-going training.

For many years Jeanne has been intimately involved with discipling students and wives at Dallas Seminary, where her husband serves as a senior professor. She travels extensively with him as part of a team and also speaks for women's conferences on her own. She has written *A Woman for All Seasons* and *Afternoon* as well as co-authored *Footprints* with her husband. Together they are general editors of *Husbands and Wives*.

INTRODUCTION

Mary Lou dropped her ballot through the slot and stepped out into the November sunshine. She had done her civic duty by voting in another election. She had tried to select candidates whose values most closely paralleled her own. As she tucked her registration card back into her billfold, she glimpsed the snapshots of her young niece and nephew. *What will the world be like for them when they are old enough to vote? And what if I have kids?* she thought. The questions fuzzed like a vapor trail in the windy sky and disappeared as she turned her car into the flow of traffic.

Mary Lou is the free world's "Everywoman"—free to vote, educated to think, unencumbered enough to steer her private life. She is several million Christian women in the United States, and you and I are included. Yet with personal privileges unprecedented in all of world history we keep bumping our heads on familiar objects. We have a hard time with husbands. We resent our parents. Children are too much to handle. Our own lives are often out of focus. We try to glorify yesterday, excuse today, and forget about tomorrow.

When the United States made its debut on the world scene, observers were agog. The fledgling British colonies had flexed their muscles and created a new nation for all to admire. Alexis de Tocqueville came to visit when our country was less than half a century old, and in 1830 the French historian published his commentary, *Democracy in America.* When asked to what he attributed our phenomenal success, he replied, "To the exceptional character of American women." Why was that true? What was so unique about the early pioneer mothers?

American women walked through the door of New World opportunity with their eyes fastened on the future. Learning from the failures of their recent past, they brought a vision of freedom based not on personal gain but on pursuit of a quality of life that deserved God's approval. They established homes and schools; they listened to men like the Reverend Cotton Mather who preached, "Ruin families and you ruin all." We know from the names of their children, their needlework, and their diaries that mothers of the Bible were their examples.

Early American women lived life in forward gear. Although they were fueled by the ancient legacy of the Judeo-Christian ethic, they assembled out of the essence of their womanhood a framework for future generations. They capitalized on their inherent ability to nurture and produced our grandmothers and great-grandmothers whom we rightfully hold in high esteem.

Somehow we seem to have misplaced the original patterns, and our inheritance stands in jeopardy. But are the biblical models still relevant for the late twentieth-century? A review of the Scriptures shows those women rising from troubling circumstances not unlike our own to places of influence and honor. We cannot ignore their parade across the pages of God's Word; they teach us how to be, and not to be, effective mothers.

I have been overwhelmingly blessed. God has graciously given me a loving husband and four children. He has sent five beautiful granddaughters who are healthy and cheerful. But He has also chosen to give me three miscarriages, to allow the strong wills of my family to clash sometimes with my own, and to take away my first grandson as a stillborn infant. It is as if the heavenly Father has said, "I love you so much that I must allow you to be hurt sometimes to help you see Me as I really am, to experience My comfort, My steady hand, My voice in the storm." I am convinced that no other curriculum could teach God's lovingkindness more effectively than that of mothering.

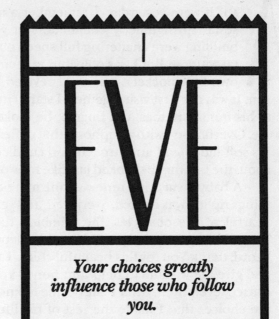

EVE

Your choices greatly influence those who follow you.

As if it were yesterday, I remember a moment of personal springtime. Jackhammers at work on a new building were chattering full speed outside my hospital window. But I was oblivious to them because in my own little pocket of privacy I reveled in my newborn son. It was our first visit together; I stared in loving wonder at his miniature toes and fingers; he looked wide-eyed at me. Overflowing with a euphoria that defies words, I kissed his soft little head and stroked and cuddled him. I mused about the fact that he looked just like my wonderful daddy.

A baby is surprise, renewal, one more chance to make things right. I was excited, overjoyed, and yet terribly afraid. Fearful of the obstacles, the enemies, the unknowns, I hugged him gently and prayed from the depths of my being, "Lord, thank You for this beautiful child. Take care of him, and give me wisdom to help him honor You." Somehow I sensed, even then, what I later came to know more surely: the choices that I made the rest of my life were going to affect my child.

I had no idea of how much I would laugh and cry and cower and, yes, despair along the path ahead. Today that young man is a thirty-seven-year-old minister of the gospel. In His infinite omniscience God answered my prayer far beyond my highest expectations and in the process taught me critical truths about myself and about Himself.

Eve was the first woman and the first mother. Her choices helped to shape those of her children; her story illustrates just how significant those choices can be.

The Divine Diary

Eve's home was no less than the Garden of Eden. God gave her everything, unblemished and perfectly balanced. But when the Tempter suggested that she lacked one particular (but forbidden) fruit, Eve elected to ignore what was right in favor of what was appealing. She allowed the Deceiver to think for her.

The distorted echoes of Eve's willful choice against

God reverberated in the lives of her children, Cain and Abel. God has given us a close-up look at what occurred in the generation immediately following Adam and Eve in Genesis 3 and 4. Observe these scenes for yourself by reading those chapters.

1. What was the crux of the argument between Cain and Abel? (Genesis 4:1-8)

2. a. How do you think Eve might have felt as this sibling rivalry developed?

   b. What consequences were hers to endure as the result of Cain's rebellion?

3. The New Testament gives us insightful commentary on the dynamics at work in the two young men. Read the following references and summarize the thought of each.

Hebrews 11:4

1 John 3:11-12

4. Every child is responsible for his own decisions. Yet how is Cain's willful choice similar to the disobedience of his parents?

5. After the family tragedy, Eve might well have given up in despair. But the fourth chapter of Genesis ends on a very hopeful note. Read Genesis 4:25. How might this new development have been used of God to encourage Eve?

Living the Truth
To understand Eve is to take the first step toward discerning myself. I am Eve's daughter, heiress to her strength as well as her disobedience. Her life and the lives of her children remind me of the importance of choosing to believe and obey God.

6. Even though the consequences of acting on our own may be disastrous, what has God promised? (Lamentations 3:21-24)

7. a. Have you made a poor decision for which you've suffered distressing consequences? What have you learned through the experience?

   b. How have you seen God's grace in spite of your failure?

8. The prophet Moses teaches us to look ahead as well as to learn from the past. For parents listening to him, what instruction and encouragement did God command Moses to give? (Deuteronomy 4:29-31)

9. Each of us can identify children or young people in our lives who are likely to imitate our faith.

   a. Name the dominant influence you are now in the process of leaving behind, after God takes you out of the picture.

   b. What spiritual heritage do you desire to pass on to the next generation?

Eve's experience ranges from highest perfection to deepest despair. Through her, we learn of God's supreme righteousness and His never-failing kindness. Eve knew both, and through her life, we may also understand His nature more clearly.

The Legacy of Eve

You and I have inherited Eve's fallen nature, but we also have been granted her sources of supply: God's presence and our own capability to decide what we will do with what we have. Often, as privileged women who nurture young people, we find ourselves frustrated when those growing lives for whom we are responsible become caught in the traps of human experience. We feel powerless and panicky, even as Eve must have felt when she watched her sons disagree and feared for their future.

Have you ever spent a night—or longer—experiencing feelings of helplessness? Have you watched a sick child with apprehension and perhaps even terror gnawing at your heart? I recall such a night when our fifteen-month-old son had drunk a large quantity of kerosene. With all his strength he had fought the hospital's stomach pump, and as he lay limply on the sheet, I could see ugly bruises marking his delicate little body. I barely noticed the night nurses as they came and went; I sat beside him replaying in my mind the doctor's words: "We've done all we can, but we expect him to contract chemical pneumonia. We'll just have to wait and see." The hardest part about waiting is that doubts begin to creep in. My mind was soon filled with them: *Does God see me here? Does He really care about my anguish? Is He punishing me for negligence? How will He choose to answer my prayers?* I tried to suppress the most painful thought: *Will I be planning a funeral tomorrow?* I struggled to think positively, but my agony persisted.

Reflecting now on that crisis, I remember that God seemed far away. He wasn't, of course, but I cowered in a defensive posture. I know I wouldn't have hurt so badly if I had remembered God's words instead of the doctor's, if I had embraced the hurt and accepted what I already knew— His mercy never varies. He always does what is in my best interest. He acts in perfect love.

God allows us—His weary, wounded, grieving children—to lay all our burdens and cares on Him ("Come to me, all you who are weary and burdened, and I will give you rest" [Matthew 11:28]; "Cast all your anxiety on him because he cares for you" [1 Peter 5:7]). When we face potentially destructive odds in our lives, Jesus Christ invites us to let Him carry the load (Matthew 11:28-30).

In such times I suggest a prayer with four petitions:

1. Dear Lord, show me what resources I have.
2. What are my alternatives in this situation?
3. Please, Holy Spirit, guide me to the best option. Show me why I should choose it.
4. Heavenly Father, I trust You to show me what to do next. Thank You for Your never-failing kindness.

Life involves a series of choices. Because decision making is such a routine part of life, I sometimes forget that every course of action I select affects some young imitator. Eve reminds me that I live by trial and error, and I need to learn instead to live by trusting God. Skillful living starts with hearing—and obeying—God's commands.

A TRIBUTE

M other was an unusual woman among others of her generation. A university graduate who also attended biblical seminary, she got married at age thirty-one and had nine children.

Mother had a great sense of humor, a deep commitment to Christ, and a very down-to-earth Christianity. She was uniquely dedicated to raising her family to the glory of God. She felt that mothering was second to none in terms of her personal priorities. Our spiritual formation was the major focus of her time, energy, and life. All her children have continued to work with the Lord; six serve Him in full-time ministry.

I believe that each of us felt that he or she was Mother's favorite because she had a way of making us feel special. She had high expectations for us, but she instilled a sense of self-confidence by her continual affirmation.

We developed a tremendous appreciation for the beauty of nature because Mother was always pointing out to us the curve of a tree trunk, the texture of the bark, the shape of a leaf, or the clouds in the sky. Everywhere we looked we'd see God because she invested nature with its true significance.

Mother would encourage us to take "memory pictures." She would ask us to note all we saw, smelled, felt, and heard. Then six months or a year or ten years later she would ask us to recall that special occasion. We could usually remember the details of those magic moments. I can remember driving off the ferry in the San Juan Islands on a beautiful summer evening as the sun was setting. My "memory picture" is still vivid even though that was forty years ago.

Another quality I appreciated about her was the honesty with which she spoke about her struggles in being a

19

mother of a family of nine children. Thousands across the country know her as the mother who wrote a monthly column in *Moody Monthly* called "Out of the Mixing Bowl." She openly shared the loneliness, frustration, and sometimes outright exhaustion of being a mother. Yet her deep trust and love for her heavenly Father always seemed to be there in the midst of the struggle. Nothing mattered more to her than pleasing Him.

Joseph C. Aldrich
President of Multnomah School of the Bible

2

SARAH

God often uses people closest to your heart to develop your faith in Him.

Alice did not know until her teen years that Walt and Ella were not her real parents. It was a family secret, one of those shameful stories that relatives agree not to discuss. Actually, Alice's mother had left home; and since she never came back, no one ever spoke of her, and the specific reasons for her leaving are lost. But Alice knew there was some reason why she was always required to do more work, dirtier jobs, with less appreciation than anyone else.

One day she met Will, the charming youngest son of a prosperous neighboring farmer. His six-foot-plus frame dwarfed her tiny work-worn body. She was not beautiful, but she was gentle and unpretentious. His family disapproved of her and made good their threat of disinheritance when Will married his Ali.

Ali was my grandmother. My clearest memory of her is a snapshot of their fiftieth wedding anniversary celebration. All dressed up, she looked like a visitor seated on the velvet sofa in the parlor of her big white farmhouse. But when the family began to sing her favorite hymn, she joined in—no, she led, because she alone knew all the words:

> Just a few more days to be filled with praise,
>   And to tell the old, old story;
> Then when twilight falls, and my Savior calls,
>   I shall go to Him in glory.
> I'll exchange my cross for a starry crown,
>   Where the gates swing outward never;
> At His feet I'll lay every burden down,
>   And with Jesus reign forever.[1]

Until Will came into her life, Ali knew little about love. But "Wild Bill," as he was known because of his skill in breaking horses, learned about life by the sweat of his brow, like Adam many millennia before him. Harsh weather, stubborn animals, and poor crops sent him looking for solutions. He knew how to farm; Ali knew how to raise chickens and plant gardens and cook for hired hands. But they learned how to love God at the little Methodist church in town. A firm belief took root: God is good, He forgives sin. The message was preached, studied, prayed, and sung. It united the family in love as they worshiped God together.

My grandmother's faith has had a profound effect on my life today. Her faith expressed itself in her choices—of love over bitterness, of gratitude and expectancy toward God over discontent and a spirit of revenge. Because of her, my own childhood was perfumed with affection and acceptance.

Somewhere in my grandmother's life, a conscious act of her will turned her toward God and changed forever the spiritual fortunes of herself and her progeny. So it was with Sarah, who had a different story but a similar brand of faith.

The Divine Diary

Sarah was the wealthy and beautiful wife of Abraham. At the very time when she should have been able to settle into a life of ease and leisure, though, God told her husband to set out for an unknown "promised" land.

From that point on, Sarah spent most of her life on the move. But her real heartache was this: she was barren, she had no child. Though God had promised Abraham descendants as numerous as the stars, Sarah was still childless when she celebrated her ninetieth birthday.

As is the case for most of us, Sarah's family relationships affected her faith. Her marriage and her longing for children nourished the development of her relationship with God. You can trace her pilgrimage by reading chapters 12, 15, 16, 17, and 21 of Genesis.

1. Out of the black confusion of a polytheistic and polygamous world stepped a man named Abraham who was committed to one God and one wife. Though far from perfect, Abraham was nevertheless an unusual man for his day.

Read and consider Genesis 12, which records an unprecedented series of events. How do you think Sarah might have felt in the various predicaments described there?

2. God's promise to give Abraham a son became Sarah's great concern. But many years had passed since that promise was made and, still, no son.

   a. Read Genesis 16:1-6 and identify what steps Sarah took as she tried to force God to perform His will on her terms.

   b. What relationships did she injure as a result?

24

3. Even after Ishmael was born, God reconfirmed His promise that Abraham would indeed have a son by Sarah (Genesis 17:15-16).

   Read Genesis 18:1-15 to discover Sarah's reaction to the Lord's promise of a son. What was her response, and what attitude do you think prompted that response?

4. Often God gives us visual glimpses of a truth He is trying to demonstrate in our lives. Abraham (and Sarah, either in person or via Abraham's recollection) witnessed, in the destruction of Sodom and Gomorrah, an extraordinary display of God's faithfulness to His Word.

   a. Read Genesis 19:27-29. What effect would this event have had on the development of Sarah's faith as she waited on God to fulfill His promises concerning a son?

   b. The birth of Isaac was another demonstration of God's faithfulness. Read Genesis 21:1-7. How would you describe Sarah in this scene?

5. The New Testament gives us even more insight into the dynamic changes that occurred throughout Sarah's life. How is she commended in these verses?

Hebrews 11:11 (NASB or NKJV)

1 Peter 3:5-6

6. Take some time to reflect on Sarah's growth as she changed from the young wife who left Haran with an entourage of relatives and servants into a mature woman of faith.

   a. How would you describe her development in faith and maturity?

   b. What propelled her forward in her life of faith?

Living the Truth

More lines of print in the Bible are devoted to Sarah than to any other woman. The New Testament commends her as a "holy woman of old" and places her in the steller roster of God's who's who of faith.

Considering the stage in which God placed her, Sarah could easily have relaxed with her charms and caprice. Instead, her life provides a classic study of the anatomy of belief. Her attitudes and conduct were developed in two critical areas: her marriage and her motherhood.

7. Sarah's faith was nurtured in the context of her family relationships.

   a. As you consider your relationships with your husband and/or with your children, what lessons of faith has God been teaching you?

   b. In the process, what glimpses has He given you of His faithfulness?

8. Like all husbands, Sarah's husband, Abraham, had his own set of weaknesses and failures. In those times when a husband's shortcomings seem to be more evident, where should a wife fix her focus? (1 Peter 3:1-6)

9. Sometimes it's hard to be patient, to trust God when we don't understand all that's happening in our family relationships. Certainly, Sarah knew the difficulty of such faith-stretching times. How do these verses encourage you as you grow in your ability to trust God?

   Romans 8:24-25

   Hebrews 11:1

10. Faith comes by hearing and heeding the Word of God (Romans 10:17). Would some aspect of your faith development as a wife, or as a mother, be enhanced by a mini-study of some specific topic in the Bible or some Bible character? If so, what (or who) would that be, and how would you go about such a study?

The Legacy of Sarah

Sarah conveys to me an exceptionally powerful message. She tells me that God takes pleasure in, and responds to, two crucial love affairs. The first is with Himself. Apart from believing (and I cannot believe without loving Him), there is nothing of lasting value I could hope to give to my children. Sarah teaches me that there is only one way to pave the future path for my children with blessing: I must believe exactly what God has said.

The second love affair is with the man God gave me. His human nature challenges my own pride. Yet as I submit to God, so must I submit to, respect, and love my husband. The two relationships go together; they must blend in my life, if my children are to learn from me how to build a life with eternal value.

Sarah stands as living proof that God is totally trustworthy. She reminds me that though others may fail me, God will not. Joshua summed it up in this succinct verse: "You know in all your hearts and in all your souls that not one word of all the good words which the LORD your God spoke concerning you has failed; all have been fulfilled for you, not one of them has failed" (Joshua 23:14, NASB).

Note
1. Charles H. Gabriel, "Where the Gates Swing Outward Never," © 1920 by Homer A. Rodeheaver.

A TRIBUTE

G rowing up in a minister's home, I became acquainted with some of the unique stresses involved in parsonage life. Of all my mother's strengths, her sense of humor added a positive dimension in our home.

My mother had a great penchant for practical jokes. For one of her favorites, she used the carpeted stairway in the foyer. She glued a nickel to a nail and then nailed the nickel into the carpet. As children, we would hide and snicker as we watched visitors try to pick up that stubborn nickel.

She saved another of her practical jokes for those times when we were entertaining dignified guests such as Vance Havner, or M. R. DeHaan, or J. Sidlow Baxter. She liked to place one of those plastic ice cubes with an insect in it in our guest's crystal water goblet. The highlight of the meal for her children was watching the guest's face as he tried to tactfully explain his dilemma to his hostess.

I remember my mother for her strength of character as well as for her sense of humor. From the age of eighteen, she had a degenerative nerve condition that totally impaired her nerve control and, to some extent, her speech. I never saw her daunted by those restrictions, however. She accepted them and proceeded with her life. I never heard her complain once about the lot that the Lord had assigned to her. Her perseverance in the midst of that daily trial was a mark of great character.

Today I find that my sense of humor is a strength in the midst of stress. My mother's example in persevering in those things that she could not control has been a great help to me as I face pressures that are sometimes beyond my control.

Joseph M. Stowell
President of Moody Bible Institute

3

REBEKAH

Those you love may suffer when you insist on your own plans.

Every mother has known failure at some time. I would like to forget, to take back my angry words, but I can never erase the distress of having bitterly told my daughter, "Do what you want to do! I know you will anyway!" Then I watched her make a critical mistake. Later she asked, "Why didn't you try to stop me?"

At the time I thought I had, but I acted in the heat of irrationality. All I could say was, "I'm really sorry, but I thought. . . ." It does not matter what I *thought*; the fact remains that I knew better, and I was weary of the struggle. I gave in, and she got hurt badly.

Other times, like Rebekah, I have tried to force circumstances to fit my wishes. Or I have done the right thing for the wrong reasons. Being a mother is tough duty, and as we'll see, God's record reminds us of the pain we can inflict on our children with "too much mothering." I gave in; Rebekah pushed too hard.

The Divine Diary
Isaac was the miracle son born to Abraham and Sarah in their old age. Isaac married Rebekah. She was a distant relative and greatly loved by her young husband. She gave birth to twin boys, Jacob and Esau.

Favoritism became a problem within the family. Isaac was drawn to the firstborn son, Esau; Rebekah loved Jacob better.

1. Read the account of this family in Genesis 25:19-28.

   a. What special information had the Lord revealed to Rebekah?

b. What may have been her reasons for favoring Jacob?

2. There was another reason why Esau had proven to be a disappointing son for Rebekah. What was that? (Genesis 26:34-35)

3. According to Old Testament law, the eldest son rightfully inherited the family birthright and blessing. Though Rebekah had the promise of God's word (that in this case the older would serve the younger), she seemed to feel constrained to help God fulfill His plan. Read Genesis 27 and observe the part Rebekah played in helping Jacob cheat his brother out of his blessing. What was her role in this devious plan? (verses 5-17)

4. a. What was the result of Rebekah's deceit in the experience of the family? (Genesis 27:41-43)

b. How might Rebekah have avoided the estrangement between her children?

Living the Truth
Rebekah had been chosen to fill a hallowed spot in Isaac's life. When he lost his mother, the presence of his wife comforted him (Genesis 24:67). Perhaps the young bride was homesick and discouraged about the expectation to live up to the legendary Sarah. Like her mother-in-law, she did not become pregnant until the Lord took away her barrenness. Her mothering was marred by playing favorites.

Whatever her reason for sowing discord in her family, Rebekah helped to rip up relationships and to bring sadness that lasted for years.

5. Rebekah loved Jacob; he was her undisputed favorite. Yet from the biblical account, we are led to believe that once he fled from Esau, Rebekah never saw Jacob again. She paid dearly for her deceit and manipulation.
God warns us not to take matters into our own hands. What insight do you receive from these verses?

Psalm 33:9-10

Proverbs 14:12

34

6. As wives and mothers, we are often greatly tempted to try to force another person's life to fit our preconceived notions of what is best.

   a. Take a few minutes to reflect on ways in which this possibility might evidence itself in your life and family. What comes to mind?

   b. As a result of observing Rebekah's life as a wife and mother, in what ways are you motivated to allow God to work toward change in your life?

7. What command does God give us as mothers who are sometimes tempted to take matters into our own hands? (Proverbs 3:3-5)

The Legacy of Rebekah

Dishonesty always reaps distress. Mistakes made by mothers seem to be particularly deadly, because they are trusted so instinctively. Mothers are meant to be the guardians and restorers of relationships within a family. Rebekah abdicated that responsibility by setting deceitful havoc in motion. Her entire family suffered the ill effects, and Rebekah lost much more than she gained. Her example warns us of the dangers of running ahead of God, not waiting for Him to act.

In some cases, the harmony we seek with our children first needs to be restored, as much as possible, with our parents. Many of us carry a grudge against one parent or the other that ties our relationships in knots and follows us to our grave. I determined that this would not happen to me as I sensed the weakening of my aged, widowed mother. I insisted that she come for an extended visit to our home in Dallas; it had been years since we had spent time together that was truly meaningful and unrushed.

Mother came in God's good timing, for the final six weeks before He called her home. We reminisced and laughed and hugged as we enjoyed each other.

Making peace is the essence of trusting God in relationships. Jesus blessed the peacemakers (Matthew 5:9). He taught us that even when we have been wronged, we are to take whatever steps we can to heal the schism and restore harmony (Matthew 18:15). A thoughtful study of Rebekah's family leads us to ask this question of ourselves: What am I doing about making peace in my family?

A TRIBUTE

Mother's strong Christian faith—my dad's, too—saw them through thick and thin. Mother had an amazing ability to stretch a dollar. Even during the depression years she managed to care for five children well, and somehow we never became anxious or felt deprived.

I think, too, of her capability to work hard without self-pity. Monday was laundry day, and she never went to bed until the last shirt was ironed, which sometimes was early Tuesday morning.

She had a tremendous steadiness under pressure. Dad was a traveling salesman, and Mother was really responsible for raising us without him. Yet where Mother was, there was always laughter. She never lost her sense of humor.

My most significant memory of her is that of the evangelistic service where I gave my heart to the Lord. As soon as I knelt, my mother was there kneeling beside me. Then, as in so many times in my life, her presence provided the comfort and encouragement that spurred me forward.

Dr. Raymond Ortlund
Former pastor
Director of Renewal Ministries

My father was a U.S. Army general, and my mother was a general, too. At least, she was every bit the strong-minded administrator that Daddy was. And all four children inherited that quality from them.

From the time both of my parents came to Christ (when I was six), Mother had an intense love for God's Word that never waned. Her unvarying habit was to get up early each morning to prepare for the Bible classes she taught for over forty years. Now all her children love the Scriptures and teach them, too.

Mother was intensely a *lady*. She taught her children

carefully—not only the Bible but also protocol, proper grooming, table manners, and so on. Recently, we three sisters were in Washington, sitting on the grass watching a parade. It's been almost half a century since Mother dressed us, but we discovered that for all our casual cottons, we had on skirts—and *hose*. We looked at one another, laughed, and acknowledged, "Mother!"

Anne Ortlund
Author and speaker

4

JOCHABED

A mother can make things work when she allows God to turn her fear into opportunity.

When we arrived at the mountain cabin, the sun was low in the west. We unpacked the station wagon, and my husband left with the girls to buy groceries while I got things ready in the kitchen. But our two boys could not resist the outdoors, especially the small lake nearby that was brimming from recent rains.

After a while I stepped over to close a window against the cold air, and I thought I heard someone yelling. It took me just a moment to tell that the familiar voice of my son was screaming, "Help! Help! Mom!"

Outside, I stumbled through the underbrush to the edge of the lake where Bob and Bill, hardly discernible in the dusky shadows, were attempting to navigate an old raft that was in the process of breaking up. They were awkwardly wielding makeshift paddles, but they were still some thirty yards from shore. What had been a kids' lark had turned into a potential tragedy.

I quickly assessed the situation and knew that I could not swim out to help, and it seemed too risky to suggest having them take off their heavy coats and swim in the frigid water. My assistance had to be verbal. "You'll make it! Keep paddling," I shouted, knowing full well the odds were against them.

"No! We're sinking!" they yelled back. I could see panic in the wild gesturing of my ten-year-old. I knew if one jumped off, the other would try to help him, and both of them might be lost. My own sense of helplessness turned to fierce determination. I decided I simply had to keep them paddling with coordinated rhythm.

"Bill, pull in long sweeps! Keep going, Bob, you'll make it!" I elongated the words in a pattern for them to follow. "Pull! Good! Pull! You're coming!" At fourteen, Bob was strong, but he was obviously stiff with fright. "You're gonna make it! You're almost here!" I reassured them.

The water had already covered their shoes, and I expected the old wreck to plummet to the bottom at any second. The wooden planks kept splitting off under the strain, and those horrible moments seemed like hours until they reached the shallows and clawed their way up the slippery bank.

What goes through a mother's mind when her child is teetering on the brink of disaster? Fear, to be sure; but fear that can be harnessed. Are you running scared? Is the world preying upon your child? You need to learn from Jochebed. She and her family lived in an Egyptian slave camp, and the tyrannical Pharaoh continually threatened their very existence. She had every reason to be overwhelmed by fear, but she did not allow that emotion to dominate her life.

The Divine Diary
Who was she, this heroine of a forced-labor pool? Jochebed and her husband, Amram, were descendants of the house of Levi. Levi had been born to a woman (Leah) in emotional anguish, who craved, but did not receive, her husband's love.

Proverbs tells us that the earth quakes under the response of an unloved wife (Proverbs 30:21-23). In such a woman, rage festers. The prophecy spoken of Levi's offspring (Genesis 49:5-7) and his subsequent family lineage depict individuals with forceful, defiant personalities. In the case of Jochebed and Amram, God used these qualities to provide the courage necessary to stand against incredible odds.

You can read Jochebed's story in Exodus 1:1-2:10.

1. a. What restrictions did Jochebed face as Moses' mother? (Exodus 1:15-22)

41

b. What options were open to her?

2. Read Exodus 2:1-4 and Hebrews 11:23, the New Testament commentary about this family's dilemma. How would you describe Jochebed's thinking and motivation?

3. What does the interchange between the Pharaoh's daughter and Jochebed's daughter, Miriam, tell about Jochebed's mothering skills? (Exodus 2:7-10)

4. What notable characteristic did Moses inherit from his parents? (Hebrews 11:24-27)

Living the Truth

Jochebed surely was no stranger to fear as she dared to trust God and to stand against the Pharaoh's edict by placing her baby in a basket in the Nile. But her fear motivated her to creative action.

The Bible speaks of two kinds of fear. The desirable kind is called "the fear of the LORD," which is the beginning of knowledge (Proverbs 1:7). This fear is the positive awe and reverence that man is to have for God, a recognition of His greatness that leads to worship. The other kind of fear is negative; it is cowardice that drains away the ability to think and act resourcefully. For the Christian, this incapacitating terror is conquerable.

As mothers, especially, we need to know how to face our fears and trust God to give us the courage to act when necessary. The Scriptures teach us how to escape the paralysis fear can often bring.

5. What are your greatest fears as a mother?

6. Psalm 34 is a wonderful example of how David dealt with his fears during some precarious days. Read and meditate on Psalm 34:1-7.

   a. What do you think is the relationship between the first paragraph of praise and the second paragraph of alleviated fears?

b. Look again at verses 4-7. List as many phrases as you can find that describe what it means to turn to God in your fear.

c. How does the Lord respond? What phrases are used to describe His response?

7. Jesus was never a mother, but the Bible tells us that He understands what we go through. Read Hebrews 4:14-16 and consider His high priestly role. How does this understanding increase our confidence as we turn to God for help?

8. From Jochebed's life as well as from Hebrews 4:14-16, how would you summarize what you've learned about dealing with your fears as a mother?

The Legacy of Jochebed
Often people have asked me what has been my greatest fear as a mother. My answer is too private to share with anyone except God. Yet with all the vigor of my heart, I want to proclaim to the world that God does carry a mother through such a firestorm of agony. He proves Himself to be what He promised—a shield, a refuge, a comforter, a restorer of the soul. He defangs the monster of fear.

Moses stands as a monument to his mother's courage against staggering opposition. Jochebed's dilemma seemed impossible, but with God's help, she solved it. Her example encourages me as I keep coming back to the Lord, morning after morning. And He is there, available to me and to any mother who seeks Him. He performs what He promises, and that assurance overcomes my fears. Perhaps His words to Joshua best summarize what I've learned over the years: "Be strong and courageous! Do not tremble or be dismayed, for the LORD your God is with you wherever you go" (Joshua 1:9, NASB).

A TRIBUTE

M y mother personified courage. We used to say, "For her family, she would fight a circular saw with her bare hands." Her favorite verse in family devotions was this: "Let us not become weary in doing good, for at the proper time we will reap a harvest if we do not give up."

Though we were poor, Mother's courage inspired us to keep trying. When I became an officer of a corporation, I put under my desk glass part of Kipling's poem "If": "Hold on when there is nothing in you except the Will which says . . . : 'Hold on!'" It reminds me of the strong will of my mother who through sickness and hard times kept courage alive for her five boys and her preacher husband.

Fred Smith
Dallas business entrepreneur

5

SAMSON'S MOTHER

When you trust God for success, the visible result may look like failure.

Cora was the oldest of ten children in a poor, immigrant German family. As a youngster, she worked in a cigar factory to help buy food. When she grew up, she met and married an outstanding craftsman, musician, and athlete who was both handsome and personable. But their happiness was eclipsed when, without warning, their firstborn son died at nine months of age from what today would be called SIDS (sudden infant death syndrome).

Cora's husband started drinking heavily, and as a result, his skills were in less demand. When a second son was born, Cora turned to God for protection and guidance while her husband's personal struggles continued. The father-son relationship was always strained, and even though his mother prayed diligently, the young man eloped at age nineteen to marry another teen of whom his family disapproved.

When I met Cora, she was a white-haired grandmother, calm, clear-eyed, and firm. She made no secret of the fact that she was praying for her son, and for his son—my husband. God had graciously brought her grandson to faith and to a decision to serve the Lord in a lifetime of ministry. But her son continued to live on his own terms, apart from God. She died without seeing her son come to faith.

Samson's mother, that unnamed saint of Judges 13, also lived with disappointment. Examine the jewel that shines amidst the record of Israel's national corruption; she has much to teach us.

The Divine Diary
Samson's mother knew what it was to bear and raise a child in a day of unprecedented decadence. It was a time in Israel's history that was similar to our own—"every one did what was right in his own eyes" (Judges 21:25, NASB). But Samson's parents had every reason to hope that their son would be special. Read their story and Samson's in Judges 13-16.

1. Since this woman had lived with the stigma of childless-ness, how did she likely react to the angel's visit? (Judges 13:2-3)

2. In her world, where most people ignored God, what hope did the angel give Samson's mother? (Judges 13:5-7)

3. What information did Manoah especially want from the man of God? (Judges 13:8-14)

4. The shock of having met an angel, together with the news of what was to occur, left Manoah stunned and frightened. But what was the response of his wife? (Judges 13:23)

5. a. Considering the concern that Samson's parents showed, what kind of home training do you think Samson received?

   b. What would his parents have envisioned and hoped for him?

6. Samson's parents surely must have questioned his choice of a woman for marriage. Read Judges 14:1-9.

   a. How do you think his parents felt?

   b. How did they respond?

Living the Truth

For Samson's trusting, sincere parents, their son's actions seem unfair, inappropriate, and certainly inexplicable. Very likely, these are the reasons God preserved the record. Parents through the ages have needed to be reminded of God's overriding grace as they have had to face their children's mistakes.

7. Have you been a mother long enough to have experienced some disappointment in one of your children? Or have you known someone who has? In such cases, what questions and frustrations does a parent have to grapple with?

8. A child isn't a blank slate on which we can write our wishes and life prescriptions for him or her. Each child comes with unique abilities and temperament. Samson was a headstrong man of appetite. And yet, almost in spite of Samson's weaknesses, God used him to accomplish His greater purposes.

   a. What does the New Testament tell us about how God viewed Samson's life? (Hebrews 11:32-34)

b. Why should this inclusion of Samson in the roster of faith be particularly encouraging to us as mothers?

9. In the difficult moments of mothering, from what promise in Psalm 103:17-18 should we draw hope?

10. If our focus is on the behavior or response of our children, we may indeed be disappointed. Where should the focus of our hope be?

   Psalm 34:5

   1 Peter 2:6

Unfulfilled expectations always come to us for the specific purpose of lifting our eyes to higher truth about God's resources. Obedience to God is never in vain.

11. How would you summarize, in a few sentences, what principle or principles we can learn from the example of Samson's parents?

The Legacy of Samson's Mother
The demands of motherhood are heavy, and sometimes the rewards are slim. Disappointment and disillusionment have been with many mothers until their deaths. But Samson's mother teaches us that God requires loving obedience and the relinquishing of results to Him.

Cora (whose story began this chapter) died, but her son lived on still surrounded by believing prayer from his son and his grandchildren. "Mother needed God," he concluded. He wept at her funeral and commended her faith, but he explained that he and God would "work out a deal." His pride held him back until—twenty years later—he was diagnosed as having throat cancer. When the doctors said, "Sorry, we can do no more for you," Cora's God got his attention.

How gracious is our God! After the cancer was found, He allowed time for Cora's son to hear again and this time accept the truth, "You must be born again." Four months later he was laid to rest in Arlington National Cemetery where someday he will be called forth by the risen Lord. Meanwhile, his spirit lives with Christ. God does not ignore a mother's prayers.

A TRIBUTE

My mother gave birth to me in a frontier house on a midwestern prairie. On the kitchen counter she placed a list of the ingredients necessary for my formula. At the top of the list was "prayer," and that remained at the top of her list for me throughout her life.

When I was eight, we moved from the country to the edge of town. I was transferred from a one-room school house with a total of nine students to a school that had twenty-four kids in just my room. I was overwhelmed, and I begged my parents not to force me to go back to that huge school. They said I must, so each night after I got in bed, my mother would pray with me for courage to get through another day at school. This is my first clear experience of God's answering prayer.

Mom was a quiet, hardworking, God-fearing person who loved her children, her Bible, and her plants. She was always available when we needed her. I have her to thank for firmly establishing my spiritual roots.

As the result of a stroke, my mom spent the last two years and ten months of her life in a convalescent hospital. Her right side was paralyzed, and she was unable to speak. Since my parents lived fourteen hundred miles away from me, I would visit Mom four times a year. I would go to the hospital every night to "tuck her in" as she had done for me years ago. I would read the Bible to her, we'd sing a hymn (she could sing, even though she couldn't speak), and then I'd pray for courage for her. She loved our quiet time together. Mom died only a few years ago, and I still miss her very much.

Lorne Sanny
*Chairman of the U.S. Board of Directors
of The Navigators*

6

NAOMI

Your greatest sorrows in mothering may lead to the avenue of God's greatest blessing.

Mother was fifty-five when Dad died. After thirty-eight years of good marriage, she was left with virtually no money, failing health, and depleted emotions. The stress of spending almost every cent for medical costs and the exhaustion from more than a year of round-the-clock nursing left her weary and hopeless about her future. Just weeks after Dad's funeral, she entered the hospital for surgery and announced to her three daughters that she was praying for the Lord to allow her not to wake up from the anesthetic.

She emerged from the recovery room filled with dread about what was to become of her, but already the first miracle had happened. Although she had no work experience in the commercial world, she had applied for a job before she had to be hospitalized. Amazingly, that fact directed the company to pay for all her medical expenses.

Mother slowly recuperated until she was able to sell blouses in a department store. She decided to take evening courses in banking, and a year later she became a teller in a downtown bank. There, one of her regular customers, a stockbroker, asked if she would be interested in an investment program. She shied away, insisting that her meager salary would never allow such risk, but he convinced her that a small mutual-funds plan would be prudent. Little did she realize that God was funding her future.

Ten years later Mother retired from the bank, sold her city house, and prepared to move into a small, renovated rural property. But before she moved, the elders of her church asked her to consider filling the place of a missionary in Mexico who needed a year's leave. Mother objected by saying that she spoke no Spanish and had never traveled outside the U.S., but three times they came from their prayer meetings and urged her to reconsider, assuring her that speaking Spanish was not required for the job as secretary to American missionaries. Timidly, she accepted, and her year in the tiny mountain village of Tamazunchale opened her eyes to cross-cultural needs. She actually taught the children with flannel-graph Bible stories and a limited vocabulary they learned from one another. Until her death, she continued a ministry of prayer for the people there.

Back home in her quiet rural community, Mother moved into neighborhood life, but her interests were global. Soon her lifelong dream came true when an opportunity arose to visit Israel. Due to her profitable investments, she was able to join a tour with her Bible school alma mater. The events of the high point of her life were forever preserved on the slides and tapes that she brought back and translated into a traveling ministry. Little churches in the area surrounding her hometown asked her to give her presentation; some of her listeners heard the gospel for the first time and were born again. Never had Mother known such fulfillment; God had saved the best until last.

So it was with Naomi, a young mother full of hope who encountered displacement, and the valley of death and despair; but she rebounded because she was held in the everlasting arms of God, and He never deserts His own.

The Divine Diary
With her husband, Elimelech, and two young sons, Naomi left her Judean home during a period of economic depression and settled in Moab. There her husband died and her sons married Moabite women. Ten years later Naomi's two sons died as well. Naomi faced the future, bereft of the men in her life, in a strange and heathen land.

To trace Naomi's journey from despair to renewed hope, read the four chapters that comprise the book of Ruth.

1. What were some of the tumultuous changes and losses that Naomi had to deal with? (Ruth 1:1-5)

2. From these verses, how would you describe Naomi's outlook as she faced an uncertain future? How was she feeling?

Ruth 1:6-14

Ruth 1:19-21

3. Ruth, her daughter-in-law, deeply loved Naomi and longed to remain with her. Read Ruth 1:15-18. What areas in Naomi's life must have been compelling to her daughter-in-law?

4. Naomi was especially encouraged when she discovered that Ruth had gleaned wheat from the field of Boaz, their close relative. According to Old Testament law, a close relative of the deceased husband was to marry his

widow and provide for her. What change seemed to be taking place in Naomi as time passed? (Ruth 2:18-20)

5. Reread the conclusion to Naomi and Ruth's story in Ruth 4:13-17. How would you describe Naomi as the grandmother portrayed in this scene?

6. Naomi could see only part of the wonderful blessings that God was bringing out of her sorrows. Read the genealogy of Christ in Matthew 1:5-17. What special role was God allowing Naomi's daughter-in-law, Ruth, to fulfill in His plan?

Living the Truth
Grief and loss are part of many lives. Broken dreams and dashed hopes test the basic value system of anyone, but perhaps it is especially true of a mother who sees that her highest goals for her children are never realized. The pain is unbearable without a reason, an overarching purpose, an assurance that God is in control.

7. Consider the comforting words of Christ that are spoken through Isaiah, and then again by Jesus (Luke 4:18-19) at the advent of His public ministry. Read Isaiah 61:1-3. What does God promise to those who mourn, to those who are discouraged?

8. Jesus, who sympathizes with our weaknesses because He was tested in every point as we are, offered His help for our struggles. Read Matthew 11:28-30 and identify the conditions necessary to experience His rest. What is His promise?

9. Naomi's story reminds us that life is a patchwork of suffering, joy, and blessing (Philippians 1:29). How do these verses encourage us to trust God, even in difficult times?

James 5:11

1 Peter 4:12-13

10. a. Is there a situation in your family that prods you to feel that life has been unfair, that God has dealt harshly with you?

b. How would you summarize what you've learned from Naomi's life and from these additional verses you've studied?

The Legacy of Naomi

This stalwart heroine from the dark era of the judges shines her beam of hope straight into the twentieth century. Everything she knew and loved had fallen apart. Her life was in tatters. She could have given up in disillusionment and died in Moab. She did not understand what had been going on, and she was bitter. She admitted it. But her Jehovah, the One who shepherds His flock, never abandons one of His sheep.

Naomi picked up the one remaining thread, her homeland with her people, and began to rework the tapestry of her life. God more than met her needs. He obviously loved her honesty and her resourcefulness. He had taken her sons, but He replaced them with a loving daughter and a robust grandson, the grandfather of King David. Eventually, the Lord Himself would be born through this woman's family.

My own mother's situation was somewhat similar. Her support system was stripped away, but God's design was to remold and renew her life, bringing a contentment she never thought possible. Our God is like that—gracious, compassionate, and full of mercy. As Dr. V.R. Edman said, "Never doubt in the dark what God has promised in the light."

A TRIBUTE

She was Kath to her close friends, Dearie to my father, and always Mother (never Mom) to her six children. When we raced in from school, Mother was unfailingly *there*, where we wanted her to be—a slim, very erect woman of five seven, quick and light of step, blue-eyed, with (in my childhood) piles of thick, glossy, dark hair. She rocked us when we were small, tucked us into bed at night, sang, and told stories. We begged for the ones about "when you were a little girl."

She was Katharine Gillingham, born June 21, 1899, in Philadelphia. We loved hearing about the butler who did tricks for her behind her parents' backs and about the alarmed postman who rushed to rescue the screaming child with her arm down a dog's throat—until he heard what she was saying: "He's got my peanut!"

In 1922 she married Philip E. Howard, Jr., a man who, because he had lost an eye in an accident, felt sure no woman would have him. They worked for five years in the Belgian Gospel Mission, then returned to the States when he became associate editor (late editor) of *The Sunday School Times*.

Mother's course was finished on February 7. She was up and neatly dressed in the morning (never in her life did she come to breakfast in any other way), made it to lunch with the help of her walker, lay down afterwards, having remarked rather matter-of-factly to someone that she knew she was dying and wondered where her husband was. Later in the afternoon, cardiac arrest took her, very quietly.

Each of us took a few minutes at the funeral to speak of some aspect of Mother's character. Phil spoke of her constancy and unfailing availability as a mother; of her love for Dad ("He was always my lover," she said). I recalled how she used to mop her eyes at the table, laughing until she cried at some of my father's bizarre descriptions or even at his oft-told jokes; how she was obedient to the New Testament pattern of godly womanhood, including hospitality. Dave talked about her unreserved surrender to the Lord, first of herself (at Stony Brook in New York), and then (painfully, years later at Prairie Bible Institute in Canada) of her children; of how, when we left home, she followed us not only with prayer but, with hardly a break for forty years, with a weekly letter. Ginny told how Mother's example taught her what it means to be a lady; how to discipline herself, her children, her home. Tom remembered the books she read to us (A.A. Milne, Beatrix Potter, *Sir Knight of the Splendid Way*, for example) and the songs she sang as she rocked each of us little children, shaping our vision of life. Jim pictured her in the small cane rocker in the bay window of her bedroom after the breakfast dishes were done, sitting quietly before the Lord with the Bible, *Daily Light*, and a notebook.

We think of her now, loving us with an even greater love, her poor, frail mortality left behind, her eyes beholding the King in His beauty. "If you knew what God knows about death," wrote George MacDonald, "you would clap your listless hands."

Elisabeth Elliot Gren
Author and speaker

7

HANNAH

> ***God may give you your heart's desire so that you can give it back to Him and have more than you ever dreamed.***

t was a rude shock to learn that our son was avoiding me. It was not a passing phase; it grew steadily worse, and as soon as he finished high school, he became independent and distanced himself from us, his family. Fourteen years later, when he received his graduate degree and was ordained into the ministry, I wept with joy to see what God had done.

For me, his mother, the turning point came on a dark day when I wrestled vigorously with despair and with God over my son's future. He was a lovable, sensitive boy, not above fighting with his brother, but tenderhearted and forgiving. I tried to understand that adolescence would move him toward manhood and away from me, but the hardness and insolence I saw in him deeply disturbed me.

In retrospect I can see that God dropped frequent hints of His care, but I became increasingly afraid, even feeling betrayed by God to whom I had entrusted this child even before his birth. As my anxiety swelled to near panic, I did something I had never done before; I fasted. Food was no longer as important as our son's welfare. For weeks, I spent each midday praying; it was my daily renewal time. Even my husband was too discouraged to talk about our son. One day as I rehearsed my anguish, the question came: Whose child is this?

Whose child? Not mine, really, just lent to me, a delightful sample of God's good gifts. I capitulated and changed my prayer. "Lord, he's Yours. He has always been Yours. You do with him whatever You please." But I could not resist adding, "Lord, please do not let him bring shame on Your name. Take him home first."

The Divine Diary
The time of the ancient Israelite judges was the setting for a woman who had extraordinary vision and faith to rise into the biblical limelight. Hannah lived in a polygamous relationship as one of the two wives of a man named Elkanah. Although she was the favored wife, she had no child, and

66

her heart ached to be a mother.

The times in which she lived were as desperate as her personal plight. Her nation was economically depressed, militarily weak, and spiritually decadent. Read her story in 1 Samuel 1:1-2:10.

1. At the feast in Shiloh, Elkanah asked his wife four questions. What do they reveal about the marriage and about his grasp of her concerns? (1 Samuel 1:8)

2. What made Hannah's prayer different from that of the usual downcast woman who offered God only her complaining? (1 Samuel 1:9-11)

3. After the child Samuel was born, the real costs of motherhood became evident. How did Hannah follow through on her promise to God? (1 Samuel 1:24-28, 2:18-19)

4. It could not have been easy for Hannah to leave Samuel with an elderly priest whose own sons were known as immoral young men. What do you see in her experience and her response that would have helped her to take such a difficult step? (1:27-28)

5. Look again at the words of commitment Hannah spoke to Eli (1 Samuel 1:26-28). Samuel must have witnessed the exchange. What do you think was the relationship between Hannah's commitment and Samuel's worshipful response?

6. In 1 Samuel 2:1-10, Hannah praises God, who gave her the privilege of bearing her son.

   a. What had Hannah learned about the Lord?

b. What is the focus of her praise?

7. How did God respond to Hannah's sacrificial spirit? (1 Samuel 2:20-21)

Living the Truth
Personal sacrifice and the willingness to dedicate her entire life to God as a mother are Hannah's outstanding qualities. There comes a time in every mother's life when, like Hannah, she must give her child back to God. Hannah models this example of a mother's surrendering, and she gently reminds us that we can't outgive God.

8. Hannah's example would lead us to believe that mothering is not a task reserved for the weak or the half-hearted. Do you agree? Why or why not?

9. God is the crowning example of the giving parent. He exhibits characteristics of both the perfect Father and the perfect Mother to us.

Read these verses in the light of being His child through Christ. Then reconsider them for the insights they give you as you parent your children.

A SHORT PARAPHRASE OF THE VERSE	INSIGHTS FOR ME AS HIS CHILD	APPLICATIONS FOR ME AS A PARENT
Psalm 103:13-14		
Isaiah 49:15		
Jeremiah 31:20		

10. Jesus spoke some strong words for any of us who want to see spiritual fruitfulness result from our efforts. Read Luke 9:23-24 and John 12:24 as though He spoke to us as *mothers*. If we want to see real spiritual fruit come from our lives as mothers, what does the Lord indicate is necessary?

11. Hannah's life as a mother is an Old Testament example of the kind of dying to self of which Jesus spoke.

    a. What major lesson have you learned from her?

    b. How can you apply what you've learned to your own life as a mother?

The Legacy of Hannah

Although Hannah did not have the written history of Christ's coming to earth, she believed wholeheartedly in the adequacy of God to meet her needs and to use her as His servant. In her book *Let Me Be a Woman*, Elisabeth Elliot makes this statement: "The measure of self-giving is the measure of fulfillment." No wonder Hannah could sing, "My heart rejoices in the LORD . . . for I delight in your deliverance" (1 Samuel 2:1). God delights in responding to our trust with a generous outpouring of His joy and peace of heart.

In my experience with our son's spiritual slump, I eventually reached a point where I declared hands off. Although I was desperately concerned about our son, I realized that I could become a victim, consumed by fear and lack of trust. "Your enemy the devil," writes Peter, "prowls around like a roaring lion looking for someone to devour" (1 Peter 5:8).

As I resisted the Devil, I was learning the truth of 1 Peter 5:10: "After you have suffered a little while, [God] will himself restore you and make you strong, firm and steadfast." Of course God was interested in my son, but He also wanted to produce in me a deep trust in His faithfulness.

It did not happen overnight, but relaxing my tension and reaffirming my belief that things do work together for good with God in charge strengthened me. The fact that today my son is an effective minister of the gospel is simply what God had in mind all along. Had He read my script, chances are that I would have missed out on learning some of the most beneficial lessons of my life and experiencing some of the greatest blessings He had in store.

A TRIBUTE

Mother taught me never to doubt the goodness of God. Though she had witnessed my father's death in a bombing raid, and she and her three children had spent three years in prison during World War II, the focus of her life was still the same—the goodness and the faithfulness of God.

During our years in China, I watched one missionary woman fall apart over the loss of a son. Another grieved for years over the sudden death of her husband. I wondered why my mother was so different.

God gave me the answer with dramatic force when my seventy-year-old mother visited our little family in the Philippines. When she was asked to speak to the Ministerial Fellowship of Davao City, she began, "Oh, the goodness and the faithfulness of God." She shared a few war stories to illustrate that we live in a world where evil is present, but she soon put the spotlight back on a loving and good God who never changes, who is with us in evil.

God touched many weary workers that day. "I've never heard anything like it," said one missionary, "to have a veteran who has gone through so much remind us that God is good and faithful."

Often asked why God's children have to suffer so much, Mother would use the occasion to turn the questioner's attention to the character of the God of love, who in good or bad circumstances never changes. "God is no person's debtor," she would conclude emphatically as the wrinkles in her smiling face underlined the truth that had set her free.

Kari Malcolm
Author

8

DEBORAH

*In crisis a mother's concern
may call for obedience to
God beyond her family.*

Mary was a wealthy and influential business-woman in the city of Dallas. Her company had grown into a national enterprise, grossing multi-million-dollar annual sales. Her prominence in the business community was simply an extension of a woman who primarily wanted to be a good mother.

The elegance of the corporate headquarters belied Mary's humble beginnings. From a turbulent childhood, she had trudged into a frantic urban pace as a dispirited divorcee with two young children. She was determined to break the cycle of poverty, failure, and futility she seemed to have inherited. In her youth, a brief stay with a godly grandmother had opened a window of hope in Mary's mind. She dared to explore the possibility that God really cares about people.

First on Mary's list of must-dos in Dallas was finding a church. She promptly joined First Baptist and then found a sales job with hours flexible enough for mothering. Eventually, she left her employer and started her own company, hiring housewives who needed money *and* self-esteem. Her warehouse was staffed primarily with handicapped people who wanted to work but never had a chance. Like a modern Deborah, Mary encouraged, rewarded, and motivated a growing corps of loyal business partners. From barbecues at her Texas ranch to retreats in her Colorado mountain cabin, she constantly nudged her expanding army of workers toward victory over despair and disillusionment.

Since Mary's death, a living legacy of families, business associates, and a host of grateful friends have continued to carry the torch she held high. Her words in *Women Who Win* read this way:

> Therein lies the real reason for our labor . . . as a way of life, a way of serving others as Jesus served us—a way of enriching the lives of others by our endeavors, as He has blessed and enriched us.[1]

Mary reminds me of Deborah, another mother in the Bible who was known for her courage and her concern for others. With her eyes on the needs of her times and a steady grip on her relationship with God, Deborah ventured forth.

The Divine Diary
Deborah arose as a judge and prophetess in Israel during the turbulent period of the judges. It was one of the lowest points of Jewish history, and the Israelites were long on enemies and short on courage and faith. Deborah responded to the critical needs of her time.

A judge in Israel was required to be forty years old. Deborah, then, was probably past the more demanding years of her mothering. Read Judges 4 and 5 to discover how God directed her nurturing, caring heart to opportunities beyond those in her family.

1. What role was Deborah willing to fill in her community? (Judges 4:5, 5:6-7)

2. Read the introduction, Judges 4:1-4, along with 5:6-9. What was the state of local affairs with respect to . . .

chatting on the village square?

traveling the roads?

worshiping Jehovah?

securing the countryside?

3. Reread Judges 5:6-9 and notice how Deborah describes herself. What do you think motivated her to action?

4. Deborah's ministry encouraged others to believe God and step out in faith against terrific odds. How do you see her faith evidenced in these verses?

Judges 4:8-9

Judges 4:14

Judges 5:1-2

Judges 5:31

5. How did God reward her faith? (Judges 4:23-24, 5:31)

Living the Truth
There are times in our lives when our families need our full attention. Certainly, our greatest gift to a desperate world will be stable, well-loved children who can shoulder adult responsibility.

But no matter what season of life we may find ourselves in, or how far outside our front door we venture each morning, God insists that we care about what happens "out there." He has never expressed fondness for apathy and indifference.

6. Two Old Testament prophets, Isaiah and Amos, reserved special rebuke and warning for the women of their culture. Amos referred to the women of his day as "cows of Bashan," likening them to the well-fed Samaritan women with insatiable desires.

Read and consider these prophets' warnings. What attitudes did they condemn? How do we, as modern women, sometimes reflect these attitudes?

THE ATTITUDE DESCRIBED	THE MODERN WOMAN'S PARALLEL
Isaiah 32:9-13	
Amos 4:1	

7. Caring is costly. Jesus emphasized this price tag when He told the parable of the good Samaritan.

   a. As you read Luke 10:30-37, think of a modern victim and fit yourself into the story. How did the good Samaritan demonstrate his sensitive awareness of the needs of a hurting individual?

b. When you read that Jesus said, "Go and do likewise," what specific need or individual did God bring to your mind from the pages of your life?

8. Deborah was a mother who allowed her nurturing concern to extend beyond the borders of her own family.

   a. What impending disaster is building near you?

   b. How can you allow your concern for your own child to "spill over" into involvement with the pressing needs around you?

81

9. We need God's discernment to keep us from becoming frazzled, overcommitted mothers. How do these verses encourage you as you seek to nurture the people in your life?

Psalm 16:7-8

Psalm 68:19

In our own critical times, I like to ask myself two questions:

▶ Do I grasp the truth that the world "out there" will eventually be my world "in here" if nothing is done?
▶ Do I, as a caring woman, really understand how much my children need me in their world?

The Legacy of Deborah
When days have been dragging along, our hearts may grow dull, and God sometimes sends shock waves to get our attention. It was many years ago, but I vividly recall that lazy summer afternoon when my husband was out of town and the children were counseling at camp or attending summer school. When I answered the phone, the camp director said, "Mrs. Hendricks, your Bev has just had an auto accident. We don't think it's too bad, but . . . ."

Instantly, all of life exploded into a frenzy of activity and long-distance communication. Friends, insurance policies, old-fashioned self-control, and common sense became vitally important. I desperately needed prayer—effective, fervent prayer—which cannot be manufactured in a split second.

My instinctive reaction after I had scribbled names and

numbers and hung up the phone was to pray, "Lord, whatever is ahead only You know. Please help me and lead me to do the right things." Nothing, absolutely nothing, surpasses the security of being able to call on the eternal God of all creation.

When I got to the hospital, I found my lovely eighteen-year-old daughter lying on a stretcher. Seeing her blood-matted hair, displaced teeth, and gashed chin was almost more than I could bear. The look in her eyes gratefully acknowledged my presence. She couldn't talk, but she needed no words. Motherhood at that time meant total concentration on a child, a complete immersion of myself into the young life God had entrusted to me.

God used an auto wreck to make motherhood even more significant for me. He taught me about life and love with a more advanced course in giving. Like Deborah of old, when I was surrounded by overwhelming odds, He comforted me and reinforced my trust in Him. Now when I help others, I share more meaningfully the Comforter I know personally. And I take every opportunity to pass along what I have found to be the most effective safeguards against complacency:

▶ a spirit of thanksgiving (Psalm 103:1-5);
▶ daily prayer for people in need (keep a list);
▶ active use of my nurturing skills (babysitting, counseling, responding to needs, and all forms of hospitality).

Mothers are uniquely equipped to spot needs and to sense the right ways to meet them. The best preparation for understanding human nature is bearing and rearing children. The Bible teaches—and history confirms—that nations are built on families. Godly mothers are "can-do" people.

Note
1. Mary C. Crowley, *Women Who Win* (Old Tappan, N.J.: Fleming H. Revell, 1979), page 142.

A TRIBUTE

Mother—all 114 pounds of her—and Daddy docked in Shanghai, China, in 1916. "Poor little Virginia Bell," one missionary observed. "She won't last a year." She lasted more than a year; she lasted twenty-five. She bore five children and buried one of them.

We lived in bandit country; I don't recall going to sleep without hearing occasional gunshots. At times it got pretty uncomfortable, yet I never saw either parent show fear.

Although Mother was plagued by headaches, she ran a terrific home that was something of an oasis where everyone was welcome. We always had two or three other missionaries living with us. By American standards, our home was primitive, but Mother made it homey and fun. Consequently, her four children have happy childhood memories.

When my husband, Bill, began his evangelistic ministry, we settled across the street from Mother and Daddy in Montreat, North Carolina. Our children had the privilege of having them as surrogate parents. They were strict disciplinarians, but they were fun grandparents, too. All our children say they do not know where they would be today spiritually had it not been for Mother and Daddy's influence.

Ruth Bell Graham
Author, speaker, and the wife
of evangelist Billy Graham

9

THE PROVERBS 31 MOTHER

*God's ideal mother influences
a world from her home base.*

When someone asked me recently, "What was the happiest time of your life?" I did not have an immediate answer. My childhood's moments of bliss were dampened by my fierce frustration that I could not be part of the big, important adult world. My adolescence was typically up and down, with some very delightful peaks, but more often anxiety kept me in the valleys, because I could not always live up to my own high standards. With adulthood came all the long-awaited privileges, but a hidden agenda of responsibilities emerged and demanded attention. Being on my own was not as much fun as I thought it would be. Early and middle adulthood were not unhappy, but they were times of very hard work.

If *happiness* means being contented and having a sense of inner well-being, present-day life is the winner by far. Although I was apprehensive about how I would cope with the aging process, my experience has held a fascinating surprise. The study of Proverbs 31 explains it: The quality that gives robust flavor to life is not beauty or charm. Those qualities are nice to have, but they're purely decorative and temporary. Real fulfillment lies elsewhere, and the mother of Proverbs 31 directs us to its Source. As verses 25-27 state, "She is clothed with strength and dignity; she can laugh at the days to come. She speaks with wisdom, and faithful instruction is on her tongue. She watches over the affairs of her household and does not eat the bread of idleness."

The Divine Diary
Read the entire thirty-first chapter of Proverbs. These words spoken to a prince by his queen mother are the essence of her lifetime's wisdom, and in verses 3-9 she conveys two succinct warnings and one positive instruction. She gives the advice in these seven verses so that her son may qualify as the husband of the "wife of noble character." It's significant to note that a description of a noble man precedes the remarks about the wife of noble character.

1. a. Read verses 3-9. What are the two warnings and one positive instruction this mother gives her son?

   b. Why do you think these instructions are important to future leaders?

2. Keep in mind that the description is not of a ready-made woman whose "on" switch is flipped at the wedding ceremony. These qualities are goals, inclinations toward which the bride is moving, priorities she holds and develops. What is the foremost feature this mother calls for in the relationship between her son and daughter-in-law? (verses 11-12)

3. The wife's activities begin and conclude with her family. (verses 10-29)

   a. What does she do specifically for them?

   b. What does this tell you about her priorities in life?

4. On the foundation of a strong marriage, a wife's outreach is extended. List the other people with whom she interacts. (verses 10-29)

5. What would her children have learned by her example? (verses 19-20)

6. a. What indications are given in verses 17,25-27 concerning physical and emotional health?

   b. How would her good health affect her children?

7. According to verses 28-31, what legacy does this woman leave? In other words, what will her children remember about their mother?

8. This woman's strength of character is founded on her relationship with God. As you think back over the entire passage (verses 10-31), how would you describe her character?

9. a. If you could pick one admirable trait of this ideal mother, which one would it be?

b. How would you begin to take steps in that direction?

Living the Truth
Based on the results of an informal survey I have been conducting for years, low self-esteem is probably the number-one problem among women in the Christian community. Experts such as Dr. James C. Dobson, Jr., feel

that our nation's highly materialistic value system imprisons a child in a poor self-image that can seriously impair spiritual growth. Who am I? is a question that remains unanswered for many women.

God, our Creator, not only made us, but He has the power to change our wrong perceptions. If we would know that steadying sense of adequacy as a wife and a mother, we must first receive God's declaration of our worth as His child in Christ. Consider some scriptural proofs of your vital place on this planet.

10. In Genesis, God outlines His original blueprint. Read Genesis 1:27 and 2:18-25. What is the significance of being a woman created in the image of God?

11. Human beings are made in God's image, a compliment that has been paid to no other creature on this planet. Psalm 139 is David's look into those moments when God formed him. From verses 13-16, state in your own words what God was doing in preparation for your birth.

12. What indication does the Lord give in these verses of His special, personalized love for you? What is the significance of the imagery used to describe that love?

Isaiah 40:11

Isaiah 49:15-16

1 John 3:1

13. Each woman goes through "passages" in her spiritual journey. Consider what God has taken you through in regard to experiencing His love, His validation of your worth.

a. Where have you come from and where are you now, in this process of experiencing His love?

b. How has the awareness of His love, or the lack of awareness, affected your mothering?

The Legacy of the Proverbs 31 Mother
The woman whose portrait appears in the divine manual on skillful living is a mother, a wife of highest character, a woman who lives to the glory of God. Her prominence in the book of Proverbs reveals God's view of the significance of our roles as wives and mothers.

The Proverbs 31 woman is praised for her work, her attitudes, and her relationships. The uniqueness of her life lies deeply within her heart and mind; she gives of herself to others because she is "a woman who fears the LORD." God's supernatural presence in her life makes her an extraordinary mother.

A TRIBUTE

"Carole, if God has a marriage partner for you in the future, then in God's eyes you are engaged already—so act accordingly." That was one of Mother's profound statements. She was a wise woman who had gained that wisdom by sitting often at the feet of the One who is wisdom.

Mother lived the Bible as well as taught it. I remember many mornings when I would see her coming from her bedroom with tears still wet on her cheeks. I knew she had been praying, especially for me. She influenced my life by the way her presence radiated the Lord.

Carole Mayhall
Author and speaker

10

ELIZABETH

Motherhood may require years of waiting, but God faithfully rewards patience.

Many years ago I took our children to meet their daddy at the Dallas airport, but he did not arrive from Chicago as scheduled. On the way home I assured them that Jesus was taking care of Daddy and they should go to sleep, but in my heart I panicked because he surely would have called if his plans had changed. After the children were in bed, I called the conference center where my husband had been and learned that all the participants were gone.

My first thought was that the small feeder flight into O'Hare Field had crashed. But I received no phone call, heard no news report to confirm such fears. I tried to pray but couldn't concentrate. I fumbled through my Bible until I landed on some verses in Psalm 3: "I lie down and sleep; I wake again, because the LORD sustains me. I will not fear." I did not know what else to do. Calling anyone seemed ridiculous since I had no information to share, only wild imaginings. So I crawled into bed, and somehow sleep overtook me—one of the many miracles of my life! At 4:40 a.m. the ringing phone awoke me. I was more than relieved to hear my husband ask me if I could pick him up. In record time I lugged four dead-weight piles of pillow-blanket-child to our station wagon and got to the airport.

The little plane had had engine trouble, and it had put down on a tiny runway for repairs. Since no phone was available, my husband had no way to assure me that all was well—just delayed. The heavenly Father knew that I could more effectively learn His lesson by seeing His care in action.

Godly patience is the art of letting God set the timer. Elizabeth, the mother of John the Baptist, knew what it was to wait and to trust God as she waited.

The Divine Diary
When the time came for God to present to the fallen world His beloved Son, the human race was lost in a spiritual darkness so intense that He needed a forerunner, an

announcer to alert people that salvation was at hand. To prepare this messenger, God chose an elderly couple named Zechariah and Elizabeth. The priest and his wife had lived faithfully and righteously in spite of the crushing disappointment of not having a child. Elizabeth had allowed this heartache to shape in her a core of inner strength and fortitude.

Luke chose to begin his gospel with their story. Read carefully Luke 1:5-25.

1. As an occupied nation of Rome, living furtively under the self-serving Herod in Judea, the Israelites often practiced a corrupted form of Judaism. What factors set Zechariah and Elizabeth apart from the rest? (Luke 1:5-10)

2. a. The angel's announcement also set their son apart from a normal lifestyle. What were the differences? (Luke 1:11-17)

b. When Elizabeth learned that she was going to be the mother of a special baby, how do you think she might have felt?

3. How would you describe the difference between the responses of Zechariah and Elizabeth when they heard the angel's news? (Luke 1:18-25)

4. After Mary learned she would give birth to Jesus, she went to see Elizabeth. In this scene (Luke 1:39-45), we see more of the faith that helped Elizabeth wait patiently on the Lord for those many years. How would Elizabeth's response have encouraged Mary to trust God?

Living the Truth

Patience is a virtue we attribute to Job. We admire it in others, talk about wanting it, and advise it for our hasty friends. We sprinkle references to patience in our pious writings: "Patience is a virtue." Yet we resist developing it voluntarily. As James states, patience comes only through tribulation; we have to hurt to learn it; we have to endure unpleasantness in order to be truly tolerant. (See James 1:2-4, 5:10-11.) We are not born with patience, and we take issue with having to grow it.

Elizabeth's example encourages us to take heart. She became a stronger woman and a better mother because of the years she spent waiting on God. Patience developed in her a strength and resilience that made her equal to any challenge.

5. a. Consider these classic passages about the person who waits on the Lord. You might want to write out a condensed form of each. What do you think it means to wait on God?

Psalm 27:13-14

Psalm 130:5-6

b. How would you describe the attitude and outlook of the mother who is patiently waiting on the Lord?

6. Waiting on God means that we don't demand that He fulfill our expectations in precisely the manner we might have envisioned. Where, then, do we place our hope? (Psalm 62:5-8)

7. How does God respond to those who wait on Him?

Psalm 40:1-3

Isaiah 64:4

8. a. Reflect on your experience as a mother. What obstacles or challenges do you face for which you are "waiting on the Lord"?

b. How can you personally cultivate the example of someone who waits on God?

The Legacy of Elizabeth

Elizabeth was a fearless woman. In spite of her childlessness, which was to the Israelite woman a deep distress and a suspected sign of divine disfavor, she focused on living a godly life. Luke does not record the details, but he reports the results. When the opportunity for heroism arose, Elizabeth was ready.

The fact that God chose her as a mentor for Mary elevates Elizabeth to a mother "superior." She had trained herself to be a nurturer so that she could manage her own pregnancy at an advanced age and tutor a young woman in the early stages of pregnancy at the same time. Her comprehension of the high value of a new life emerging in God's timing, her ability to rest in His perfect plan, made her the ideal mother. She and her husband, Zechariah, parented a son, John, who Christ Himself said was without equal. More than any other quality, Elizabeth teaches us the value of perseverance in righteousness.

A TRIBUTE

When I think of my mother, one particular scene comes immediately to mind. As a budding baseball player of eleven, I remember looking up into the stands on a particularly hot summer day and noticing my mother there. It suddenly struck me that she probably had better things to do, even more important things to do than to watch her son play a game she knew very little about. Yet she was there, not only that day, but many other afternoons and evenings as well. The whole idea of loyalty and commitment began to form in my mind around the image of her presence there. Loyalty and commitment transcend personal desires and comfort, and I began to learn that truth at a very early age from my mother.

Ronald W. Blue
President of Ronald Blue & Co.
Financial and investment counselors

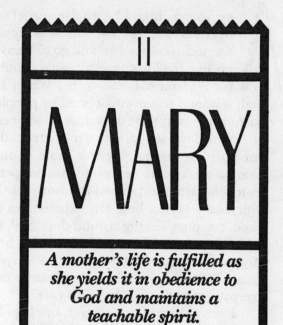

II

MARY

A mother's life is fulfilled as she yields it in obedience to God and maintains a teachable spirit.

As a young child, I heard the gospel and made a firm decision to accept Jesus Christ as my personal Savior. I wanted to escape hell and go to Heaven at the end of my life; but I felt quite sure that I could handle myself for a lifetime. I was wrong. When I reached junior high school, I was overwhelmed by people and pressures pushing me away from the values I had been taught. During one of my high school years, my parents decided to spend our vacation camping near a Bible conference. There I heard a missionary describe what happened after a German submarine torpedoed the hospital ship *Zamzam*, on which he was traveling. His experiences of being imprisoned, escaping, fleeing around the world, and finally arriving back home held me spellbound until he asked, "Is there any young person in this room who will put his or her life totally in God's hands, knowing that no matter where you are, you are perfectly safe in His care?"

I was a shy young teenager, but I could not stay in my seat. In a large church filled with people I stood and walked to the front to indicate probably the most important and far-reaching decision of my life. It was one year before my high school graduation, but it was the night I really began to live.

Mary of Nazareth, who historians say was probably in her teens, truly began to know fulfillment as well when she said yes to the proclamation of the angel Gabriel and to God.

The Divine Diary
The birth of a child is God's indication that the world must go on, but Gabriel announced the impending arrival of a special child who was to play a more far-reaching role than any other. He would strike God's mortal blow against Satan, the father of wickedness. The place, the persons, and the drama of the Incarnation highlight the significance of this event.

Read the beginning of Mary's story in Luke 1:26-56.

1. How did the angel make his message believable and relevant to Mary's experience? (Luke 1:26-37)

2. As a virgin engaged to Joseph, Mary knew that her pregnancy placed her in an awkward position. Who would understand this? By Jewish law, Joseph could divorce her for unfaithfulness. In light of this situation, what conclusion about her spiritual maturity can we draw from Mary's responses? (Luke 1:38)

3. Mary's relative, Elizabeth, was going to give birth to a special baby as well. Can you think of some practical reasons why it was important for Mary to visit Elizabeth? What would Mary have gained? (Luke 1:39-45)

4. How do the implications of Luke 1:45 apply to each of the expectant mothers?

5. Read Mary's song (the Magnificat) in Luke 1:46-55. Though Mary was just a teenager, what does this song reveal about her spiritual understanding and perception?

Living the Truth
Mary's life illustrates her stalwart dedication—no stalling, no bargaining, no evidence of retreat. Just as she did, we must choose obedience to God's will; every other choice leads to eventual loss.

Mary is one of the few biblical women we may observe in her role as a mother throughout the course of her Son's life. Let's look at her in some later episodes.

6. Mary had many heartaches as a mother. The aged and devout Simeon gave her a glimpse of what was to come. (Luke 2:25-35)

   a. What specific words did Simeon have for Mary, and how might they have affected her? (verses 34-35)

b. As Mary "treasured up all these things and pondered them in her heart" (Luke 2:19), how do you think she combined the message of the angel Gabriel and the words of Simeon? What conclusions might she have drawn?

7. Most of us as mothers have known something of that mixture of heartache and exuberant thrill. How have you seen that combination in your experience?

8. The gospels record only one incident when Jesus was a boy in the care of His parents. Read Luke 2:39-51.

a. How might Mary have felt in this situation?

b. What did she learn?

9. Mary was a devoted disciple as well as Jesus' mother. What do these scenes tell you about Mary in both roles?

John 19:25-27

Acts 1:14

10. a. What character traits are being required of you in this phase of your mothering?

b. In what ways is your obedience to the Lord exemplified by your life as a mother?

The Legacy of Mary

Mary, the mother of our Lord, has been venerated for centuries. But she, above all women, stands as a very human testimony to the value of giving one's life to God without any qualifications. Even as she had to endure the pain of misunderstanding, she was learning from her Son the truth about sin and salvation. Indeed, Mary knew the pain of the Cross in her mothering, but she also experienced the fulfilling liberty that comes only from being His devoted disciple.

Have you ever crossed a hanging bridge? On my uncle Paul's farm one led to the cornfield where we cousins loved to play. I often stood on one end gathering my courage and determination to step out, but after I started out bravely, the bouncing paralyzed me with fear and trembling. My mischievous cousin Tom delighted to see his city cousin frozen with terror, and he would jiggle the other end with all his might.

The way we look at motherhood is very much like that. Sure, we think, it won't be easy, but we're determined; we can get across. Then the shakes and shocks hit us, and we find ourselves calling out to the Lord, asking Him to quiet our hearts and steady our steps. And He does; He is the solid Rock beneath us.

A TRIBUTE

One day I returned home from school with one of those infamous notes from my elementary school teacher. I had the "gift" of talking in class and talking back to my teacher. My mother was becoming more and more frustrated by my behavior at school and her inability to change my attitude.

On this occasion she stood there with tears in her eyes, and then she led me to her bedroom. I was expecting a well-deserved spanking, but what I got was far more effective. She had me kneel down with her as she prayed and asked the Lord for wisdom to guide her son. And as she prayed, she cried. I was deeply moved. If my behavior was that important to her, I knew I had to change. No spanking I ever received had as much impact as kneeling next to my praying mother.

I will always remember my mother for her servant spirit. Our home was open to missionaries passing through our town, newcomers in our church, and hurting people. Her compassionate feelings for those people were evident in dinner-time prayers and in the contents of her oven because she was always baking something for someone. Her actions and attitudes showed how much she valued people, and that message made a lasting impression on me.

Dennis Eenigenburg
Pastor

BIBLE STUDY MATERIALS
FROM NAVPRESS

BIBLE STUDY SERIES
DESIGN FOR DISCIPLESHIP—seven books and leader's guide
EXPERIENCING GOD—two books
GOD IN YOU—six books and leader's guide
GOD'S DESIGN FOR THE FAMILY—two books
LEARNING TO LIVE—six books
LIFECHANGE—studies of books of the Bible
STUDIES IN CHRISTIAN LIVING—six books

TOPICAL BIBLE STUDIES
Becoming a Woman of Excellence
The Blessing Study Guide
Celebrate the Seasons!
The Creator, My Confidant
Growing in Christ
Growing Strong in God's Family
Healing the Broken Places
Homemaking
Justice
Leadership
A Mother's Legacy
The New Mothers Guide
On Holy Ground
Political Action
Saints, Sinners, and a Sovereign God—and leader's guide
To Walk and Not Grow Weary
Transforming Society
When the Squeeze Is On

BIBLE STUDIES WITH COMPANION BOOKS
The Freedom of Obedience
Inside Out
Living for What Really Matters
The Practice of Godliness
The Pursuit of Holiness
Trusting God
Your Work Matters to God

RESOURCES
How to Lead Small Group Bible Studies
Jesus Cares for Women
The Navigator Bible Studies Handbook
Topical Memory System—available in KJV/NIV and NASB/RSV
Your Home, A Lighthouse